The Life-Support Guide to Quit Drinking

The 9+1 Sober Tips on How to Take the Radical Choice to Stop Drinking and Fix Past Mistakes

Allison Alcantara

ALLISON ALCANTARA

"THE REVOLUTIONARY METHODS FOR ADDICTIONS"

Allison Alcantara has been a heavy smoker for over 30 years. In 1983, after countless failed attempts to quit, she went from 60-100 cigarettes a day to zero without suffering from withdrawal, without using willpower, and without gaining weight. She realized she had discovered what the world was waiting for, the easiest way to quit smoking, and she embarked on a mission to help cure the smokers of the world.

As a result of the phenomenal success of her method, she has earned a reputation as a "Cigarette Killer" and has become a worldwide expert on quitting smoking.

Allison Alcantara's "Spit-Out-It" Method has been successfully applied to a number of problems including sugar addiction, alcohol, debt, and other addictions.

Disclaimer and Terms of Use: Effort has been made to ensure that the information in this book is accurate and complete, however, the author and the publisher do not warrant the accuracy of the information, text and graphics contained within the book due to the rapidly changing nature of science, research, known and unknown facts and internet.

The Author and the publisher do not hold any responsibility for errors, omissions or contrary interpretation of the subject matter herein. This book is presented solely for motivational and informational purposes only.

Contents

Introduction

Around 2 billion individuals overall devour alcoholic drinks, which can have prompt and long-term consequences on health and social life. More than 76 million people are presently affected by alcohol use disorders, for example, alcohol reliance and abuse. Contingent upon the measure of alcohol consumed and the example of drinking, alcohol consumption can prompt inebriation and alcohol reliance. It can bring about disablement or death from accidents or contribute to depression and suicide. Moreover, it can cause chronic illnesses, for example, cancer and liver disease in individuals who've been drinking heavily for some years.

Alcohol has a toll of 1.8 million deaths every year, which addresses 3.2% of all deaths worldwide. Unexpected wounds represent about 33% of the deaths from alcohol. Alcohol is the third most basic reason for demise in developed nations. In the predetermined number of agricultural nations where mortality is low, alcohol is the main source of illness and sickness.

Damage to human existence is frequently portrayed regarding the loss of "disability-adjusted life-years" (DALYs). This measure considers the quantity of years lost because of unexpected losses just as the years went through living with a disability.

Worldwide, alcohol causes a deficiency of 58.3 million DALYs annually, which addresses 4% of the total loss of DALYs from all causes. Mental disorders and illnesses of the sensory system account for about 40% of DALYs lost due to alcohol.

Why do People drink Alcohol?

For a great many people, a drink or two can be an approach to celebrate an occasion or praise a decent meal. Others may not appreciate alcohol by any stretch of the imagination; they don't care for the taste, they don't care for the vibe of being tipsy, or they don't care for feeling out of control. In case you end up finding a way into these categories, understanding the difficult drinker in your life can be troublesome.

At Origins, we are an organization involved to a great extent of recuperated alcoholics, so we see really well why individuals drink — not just toward the start of their "drinking vocations," however whenever addiction has grabbed hold.

The "Effect Produced"

In the beginning phases of drinking, people frequently find that alcohol creates a scope of lovely effects. These effects are frequently slippery to such an extent that people keep on drinking even after their drinking has become "a problem." Here are a couple of those effects noted by both moderate drinkers and alcoholics the same.

Stress Relief

For both moderate consumers and alcoholics, alcohol has awesome anxiolytic ("anti-anxiety") properties, which means it can restrain anxiety or the sensation of stress. It is a typical path for individuals to loosen up in the wake of a monotonous day's work.

Alcoholics frequently discover this effect from the beginning in their drinking careers. As addiction takes hold, the beset person continues to drink despite evidence that alcohol is done giving any semblance of stress relief. Moved by the delusion that they can stop after a glass or two, they unsuccessfully chase this sensation of relief. As a rule, for the alcoholic, drinking alcohol exacerbates the very stress they were expecting to maintain a strategic distance from.

Peer Pressure and Camaraderie

Numerous people drink when others around them are drinking. Indeed, most non-alcoholics will in general drink in social circumstances, for example, weddings or football games, where alcohol is viewed as a piece of the actual occasion. Despite the fact that the expression "peer pressure" is regularly connected with young people, it isn't restricted to those in middle school, secondary school, or school. Drinking is pervasive in our way of life, socially acknowledged, and lawful. Peer pressure to drinking alcohol can exist at any phase of life.

For the alcoholic, the fixation to drink can transform peer pressure into a cleverly disguised excuse for drinking—in any event, when they realize they shouldn't drink dependent on mounting evidence it's an issue. Regularly, alcoholics accept they are drinking to have a good time and enjoy time with their friends which is strangely unexpected as they as often as a possible drink alone.

To Lose One's Inhibitions

Let's be honest, there are a lot of shy individuals out there. Additionally, there are likewise many circumstances in which somebody doesn't even essentially need to be too shy to be scared. First dates and enormous gatherings loaded up with strangers are common examples. Whatever the explanation, individuals regularly drink alcohol to lose their restraints in these sorts of settings. On account of alcohol's ability to cause individuals to feel great in circumstances where they in any case would not, it is commonly referred to as "liquid courage." For some non-alcoholics, it is an awesome, brief "social lubricant."

Binge drinkers may turn out to be uninhibited to such an extent that they act in an inappropriate, embarrassing, or obnoxious manner. For drunkards who have built up a staggering obsession to drink, this effect can deteriorate relationships and cause untold horror.

Alcohol

▶ Why do people drink?
- ▶ They may want to fit in with a group.
- ▶ They may want to feel older.
- ▶ They may think it will help them avoid their problems.
- None of these are healthful reasons.

Effects of Alcohol on Your Body

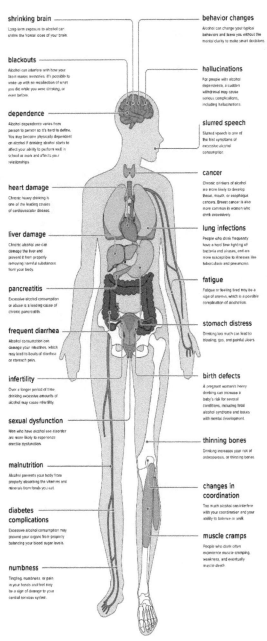

shrinking brain

Long-term exposure to alcohol can shrink the frontal lobes of your brain.

blackouts

Alcohol can interfere with how your brain makes memories. It's possible to wake up with no recollection of what you did while you were drinking, or even before.

dependence

Alcohol dependence varies from person to person so it's hard to define. You may become physically dependent on alcohol if drinking alcohol starts to affect your ability to perform well in school or work and affects your relationships.

heart damage

Chronic heavy drinking is one of the leading causes of cardiovascular disease.

liver damage

Chronic alcohol use can damage the liver and prevent it from properly removing harmful substances from your body.

pancreatitis

Excessive alcohol consumption or abuse is a leading cause of chronic pancreatitis.

frequent diarrhea

Alcohol consumption can damage your intestines, which may lead to bouts of diarrhea or stomach pain.

infertility

Over a longer period of time, drinking excessive amounts of alcohol may cause infertility.

sexual dysfunction

Men who have alcohol use disorder are more likely to experience erectile dysfunction.

malnutrition

Alcohol prevents your body from properly absorbing the vitamins and minerals from foods you eat.

diabetes complications

Excessive alcohol consumption may prevent your organs from properly balancing your blood sugar levels.

numbness

Tingling, numbness, or pain in your hands and feet may be a sign of damage to your central nervous system.

behavior changes

Alcohol can change your typical behaviors and leave you without the mental clarity to make smart decisions.

hallucinations

For people with alcohol dependence, a sudden withdrawal may cause serious complications, including hallucinations.

slurred speech

Slurred speech is one of the first symptoms of excessive alcohol consumption.

cancer

Chronic drinkers of alcohol are more likely to develop throat, mouth, or esophagus cancers. Breast cancer is also more common in women who drink excessively.

lung infections

People who drink frequently have a hard time fighting off bacteria and viruses, and are more susceptible to illnesses like tuberculosis and pneumonia.

fatigue

Fatigue or feeling tired may be a sign of anemia, which is a possible complication of alcoholism.

stomach distress

Drinking too much can lead to bloating, gas, and painful ulcers.

birth defects

A pregnant woman's heavy drinking can increase a baby's risk for several conditions, including fetal alcohol syndrome and issues with mental development.

thinning bones

Drinking increases your risk of osteoporosis, or thinning bones.

changes in coordination

Too much alcohol can interfere with your coordination and your ability to balance or walk.

muscle cramps

People who drink often experience muscle cramping, weakness, and eventually muscle death.

Alcohol's effect on your body begins from the second you take your first taste. While a periodic glass of wine with supper isn't a reason for concern, the combined impacts of drinking wine, lager, or spirits can incur significant damage.

Digestive and endocrine glands

Drinking a lot of alcohol can cause abnormal activation of digestive enzymes created by the pancreas. The development of these enzymes can prompt inflammation known as pancreatitis. Pancreatitis can turn into a drawn-out condition and cause serious intricacies.

Inflammatory damage

The liver is an organ that assists break with bringing down and eliminate harmful substances from your body, including alcohol. Long-term alcohol use meddles with this cycle. It additionally expands your danger for chronic liver inflammation and liver disease. The scarring brought about by this inflammation is known as cirrhosis. The development of scar tissue annihilates the liver. As the liver turns out to be progressively harmed, it has a harder time eliminating toxic substances from your body.

Sugar levels

The pancreas manages your body's insulin use and reaction to glucose. At the point when your pancreas and liver aren't working appropriately, you risk experiencing low blood sugar or hypoglycemia. A harmed pancreas may likewise keep the body from producing sufficient insulin to utilize sugar. This can prompt hyperglycemia or a lot of sugar in the blood.

Central nervous system

As alcohol makes more damage to your central nervous system, you may encounter numbness and tingling sensations in your feet and hands. Drinking additionally makes it hard for your brain to make long-term memories. It likewise lessens your capacity to think clearly and settle on rational decisions. Over the long run, frontal lobe damage can happen. This territory of the brain is answerable for emotional control, short-term memory, and judgment, in addition to other essential jobs.

Digestive system

The association between alcohol utilization and your digestive system probably won't appear to be immediately clear. The side effects frequently just appear after there has been damage. Furthermore, the more you drink, the greater the damage will turn into. Alcohol can damage the tissues in your digestive tract and keep your intestines from processing food and absorbing nutrients and vitamins. Subsequently, malnutrition may happen. Excessive alcohol consumption can cause the following:

- gassiness
- bloating
- a feeling of fullness in abdomen
- diarrhea

Circulatory system

Alcohol can influence your heart and lungs. Individuals who are chronic drinkers of alcohol have a higher danger of heart-related issues than individuals who don't drink. Women who drink are bound to create heart disease than men who drink. Circulatory system complications include:

- High blood pressure
- Irregular heartbeat
- Difficulty pumping blood through the body
- Stroke
- Heart attack
- Heart disease

Sexual and reproductive health

You may figure drinking alcohol can lower your restraints and assist you with having a good time in bed. However, the reality is very unique. Men who drink in excess are more liable to experience erectile dysfunction. Heavy drinking can likewise prevent sex hormone production and lower your libido.

Women who drink a lot may quit menstruating. That puts them in more serious danger for infertility. Women who drink intensely during pregnancy have a higher danger of premature delivery, miscarriage, or stillbirth.

Skeletal and muscle systems

Long haul alcohol use may keep your body from keeping your bones solid. This habit may cause thinner bones and increment your danger for fractures in the event that you fall. And fractures may recuperate more slowly. Drinking alcohol may likewise prompt muscle weakness, cramping, and eventually atrophy.

Immune system

Drinking heavily weakens your body's regular insusceptible framework. This makes it harder for your body to ward off invading germs and infections.

Individuals who drink heavily throughout a long timeframe are additionally more prone to develop pneumonia or tuberculosis than the general population. Around 10% of all tuberculosis cases worldwide can be attached to alcohol consumption. Drinking alcohol likewise builds your danger for a few kinds of cancer, including mouth, breast, and colon.

Effects of Alcohol on the Body

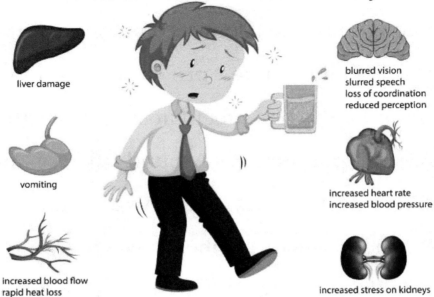

liver damage

vomiting

increased blood flow
rapid heat loss

blurred vision
slurred speech
loss of coordination
reduced perception

increased heart rate
increased blood pressure

increased stress on kidneys

What is Alcoholism

Alcoholism is the most dangerous type of alcohol abuse and includes the inability to manage drinking habits. It is likewise usually alluded to as alcohol use disorder. Alcohol use disorder is coordinated into three classifications: mild, moderate, and severe. Every classification has different symptoms and can cause hurtful side effects. Whenever left untreated, any sort of alcohol abuse can spiral crazy. People battling with alcoholism regularly feel like they can't function typically without alcohol. This can cause alot issues and affect professional objectives, individual issues, relationships, and by and large wellbeing. Over the long haul, the genuine side effects of predictable alcohol abuse can deteriorate and deliver harmful entanglements.

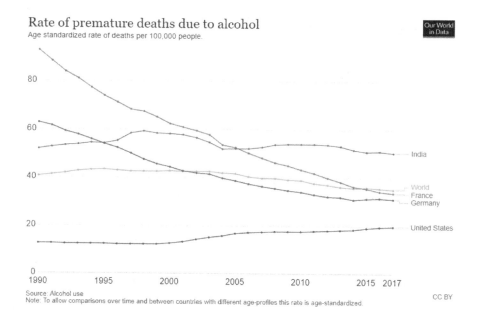

Rate of premature deaths due to alcohol
Age standardized rate of deaths per 100,000 people.

The chart shows alcohol consumption since 1890 out of various countries. Across these high-income countries, the annual average today lies between 5.6 liters in Japan and 10.4 liters in Austria. A century ago, a few countries had a lot higher degree of alcohol consumption. In France, during the 1920s the average was 22.1

liters of pure alcohol per person per year. This equivalents 184 one-liter wine bottles per person per year. Note that as opposed to the cutting edge insights that are communicated in alcohol consumption per person older than 15 years, this incorporates children also – the average alcohol consumption per adult was therefore much higher.

Types of Alcoholism

Various kinds of alcoholics will languish over various reasons. A few gatherings may not understand that their drinking is an issue. Or maybe, it is only a piece of what their identity is. Notwithstanding, regardless of your age, status, or family, alcoholism can make long-term issues that damage your health and relationships, regardless of the subtype. There is a generalization in America of a "typical alcoholic". Nonetheless, an investigation from the National Institute on Alcohol Abuse and Alcoholism (NIAAA), National Institute of Health (NIH), and the National Epidemiological Survey on

Alcohol and Related Conditions (NESARC) set out to settle that notion. These organizations conducted a national, clinical investigation got from different examinations on alcoholics. The examination found that there are five subtypes of alcoholics which are the following:

Young Adult Subtype

It is resolved that generally 31.5% of alcoholics fall into youthful grown-ups, which is the biggest single gathering. This gathering will in general start drinking at an early age (around 19) and builds up an alcohol reliance ahead of schedule (around 24). This gathering has nearly low paces of co-happening psychological wellness conditions and moderate paces of other substance misuse issues and relatives with alcoholism. The youthful grown-up subtype is less inclined to make some full-memories work however is bound to be in school than different gatherings.

This gathering is likewise far-fetched at any point to have been hitched. This subtype drinks less often than others however is probably going to take part in binge drinking when they do. Individuals from this gathering are 2.5 occasions bound to be male than female.

Functional Subtype

The Functional subtype is your opinion about when you hear "functional alcoholics." Making up 19.5% of alcoholics, this is the gathering that is holding down positions and connections. This gathering will in general be moderately aged (around 41). Individuals from this gathering for the most part begin drinking later (around 18) and create liquor reliance later (around 37). This gathering experience moderate paces of depression however lower paces of most other co-happening issues. Numerous individuals from this gathering smoke cigarettes, however few have other substance use issues. Around 60% of this gathering are male.

Of all subtypes, the functional subtype is the to the least extent liable to have lawful issues, and they are the most drastically averse to report issues because of their drinking. They have the most noteworthy education levels and pay of a wide range of alcoholics. A big part of this gathering are hitched. These are individuals that may appear to have their coexistences, the ones that others gaze upward to. Be that it may, while they are "functional" it might be said, they are as yet experiencing compulsion.

Intermediate Familial Subtype

The intermediate familial subtype represents 18.8% of alcoholics. This gathering will, in general, beginning drinking younger (around 17) and builds up a liquor reliance prior (around 32). This subgroup is probably going to have had close family individuals with alcoholism. They also have a high likelihood of experiencing an enemy of social character problems, depression, summed up uneasiness, and bipolar issues. This gathering additionally experiences high paces of cigarette, marijuana, and cocaine compulsion.

The intermediate familial subtype is 64% male. This gathering has an advanced education level than most, yet not as high as the practical subtype. More individuals from this gathering have everyday positions than some others. However, their pay level will, in general, be lower than the utilitarian subtype. While this gathering isn't particularly prone to look for treatment, those that do will, in general, go-to self-improvement gatherings, strength treatment programs, detoxification projects, and private medical care suppliers.

Young Antisocial Subtype

21.1% of alcoholics fall into the youthful antisocial subtype. In general, this gathering will begin drinking at the youngest age (around 15) and builds up a liquor dependence at the most punctual age (around 18). Over half of this gathering have characteristics of against social character issue. They also have high paces of depression, bipolar confusion, social fear, and the top urgent problem. Likewise, this gathering has the most elevated paces of other substance misuse problems, including dependence on cigarettes, weed, meth, cocaine, and narcotics. More than 3/4 of the individuals from this gathering are male. This gathering has the most minimal degrees of education, work, and pay of any gathering. This gathering likewise drinks more at one time and more generally speaking than another gathering, even though they drink marginally less oftentimes. Then again, this gathering is bound to look for help than practically some other, with 35% having searched out some help with defeating alcoholism. This gathering has the most noteworthy pace of looking for treatment from a private medical care supplier, yet additionally frequently picks self-improvement gatherings, strength therapy projects, and detox programs.

Chronic Severe Subtype

The persistent extreme subtype makes up the littlest level of alcoholics, with just 9.2%. This gathering will, in general, beginning drinking at a youthful age (around 15); however, it commonly builds up an alcohol dependence at a moderate age (around 29). 77% of this gathering have close family individuals with alcoholism, the most elevated level of any subtype. 47% of the individuals from this gathering display hostility to social character issues, the second most elevated pace of any subtype. This subtype is the most probable of any to encounter significant depression, dysthymia, bipolar turmoil, summed up nervousness problem, social fear, and frenzy issue Likewise is this gathering e, is probably going to encounter dependence on cigarettes, marijuana, cocaine, and narcotics. Over 80% of these gathering encounters intense alcohol withdrawal and persevering endeavors to chop down. Over 90% experience drinking despite the issues it causes them and drinking bigger sums and for more than planned. This gathering, likewise, will, in general, invest critical measures of energy recuperating from alcohol, and many experiences decreased exercises because of drinking. This gathering additionally sees the most elevated pace of trauma center visits because of drinking. This gathering has the most elevated paces of separation and partition.

Causes of Alcoholism

Alcohol use disorder (AUD) can come from various components. After an extensive stretch of drinking, your mind starts to depend on alcohol to deliver certain synthetic compounds. This is the thing that makes it hard for hefty drinkers to stop and can cause awkward withdrawal indications.

Here's a breakdown of how each one performs a function within the development of alcohol abuse.

Alcohol use disorder (AUD) can come from different factors. After an extensive stretch of ingesting, your cerebrum begins to depend upon alcohol to deliver certain chemicals. This is the thing that makes it hard for alcoholic give up and can cause uncomfortable withdrawal signs and symptoms. Numerous of the maximum not unusual reasons of alcoholism are:

- Biological factors

- Environmental factors

- Social factors

- Psychological factors

Here's a breakdown of how everyone assumes a part in the development of alcohol abuse.

Biological Factors

Research has shown a nearby connection between alcoholism and biological factors, especially genetics and physiology. While a few people can restrict the measure of alcohol they devour, others feel a strong impulse to continue onward. For a few, alcohol radiates feelings of pleasure, encouraging the brain to rehash the conduct. Dreary conduct like this can make you more vulnerable to developing alcoholism. There are likewise sure chemicals in the brain that can make you more helpless to alcohol abuse. For example, scientists have demonstrated that alcohol dependence might be related to up to 51 genes in different chromosome regions. In the event that these genes are gone down through generations, relatives are significantly more inclined to developing drinking problems.

Environmental Factors

As of late, studies have investigated a potential association between your environment and the danger of AUD. For example, numerous researchers have analyzed whether an individual's nearness to alcohol retail locations or bars affects their odds of alcoholism. Individuals who live nearer to alcohol establishments are said to have a more uplifting point of view toward drinking and are bound to take an interest in the action. Moreover, alcohol manufacturers are assaulting the overall population with advertisements. A significant number of these advertisements show drinking as a satisfactory, fun, and loosening up diversion. In only forty years – somewhere in the range of 1971 and 2011 alcohol promotion in the US expanded by in excess of 400 percent.

Another environmental factor, pay, can likewise assume a part in the measure of alcohol an individual consumes. In opposition to prevalent thinking, people who come from wealthy areas are bound to drink than those living beneath neediness. Gallup's new yearly utilization propensities survey showed that about 78 percent of individuals with a yearly family pay of $75,000 or more consume alcohol. This is fundamentally higher than the 45 percent of individuals who drink alcohol and have a yearly family pay of under $30,000.

Social Factors

Social factors can add to an individual's perspectives on drinking. Your culture, religion, family, and work impact large numbers of your behaviors, including drinking. Family assumes the greatest part in an individual's probability of developing alcoholism. Kids who are presented to alcohol abuse since the beginning are more in danger of falling into a dangerous drinking pattern.

Psychological Factors

Diverse psychological factors may build the odds of heavy drinking. Each individual handle circumstance in their own interesting manner. Nonetheless, what you adapt to these sentiments can mean for certain behavioral traits. For instance, individuals with high stress, anxiety, depression, and other mental health conditions are more defenseless against developing alcoholism. In these sorts of conditions, alcohol is regularly used to stifle sentiments and ease the symptoms of psychological disorders.

Alcoholism Risk Factors

There are many risk factors engaged with the potential for developing alcoholism. Alcoholism risk factors don't mean you will develop a drinking issue; in any case, they should fill in as a prevention measure. In the party that you have at least one risk factor, talk with a medical health professional about alcoholism warning signs and prevention assets. A few basic alcohol misuse risk factors are the following:

Drinking at an Early Age

Drinking with alcohol at a young age can prompt issues later on throughout everyday life, particularly in your 20s and 30s. This is particularly obvious when adolescents engage in incessant binge drinking. While drinking from the beginning can increase the probability of alcohol abuse, alcoholism can influence anybody at any age.

Family History with Alcohol Addiction

Growing up around relatives and close family members that experience the ill effects of heavy alcohol increases the risk of alcohol abuse for the next generations to come. At the point when you're encircled by individuals who drink unnecessarily, you can see alcohol use contrastingly and succumb to unfortunate propensities.

High Levels of Stress

Drinking with an end goal to lessen stress can rapidly turn tricky. Career ways that are bound to confront significant degrees of stress because of extended periods and strenuous undertakings incorporate doctors, nurses, emergency rescue workers, construction workers, and the military. It's significant for experts of any industry to discover alternative approaches to destress to forestall alcohol abuse.

Peer Pressure

At the point when a partner or dear companion every now and again drinks, you might be more disposed to go along with them. Surrendering to peer pressure can prompt drinking issues as it were, just as numerous unexpected issues that emerge from over-the-top alcohol utilization. As opposed to wanting to drink, offer to be a designated driver.

Frequent Alcohol Consumption Over a Long Period

When drinking an excessive amount of turns into an example, you significantly increase your odds of building up an alcohol-related issue. The more you drink, the more your body fabricates a resistance to alcohol. Resilience implies you'll require more alcohol to feel similar affects you used to feel with less.

Mixing Alcohol with Other Drugs

Drinking alcohol to intensify or descend off the high of different drugs, for example, prescription opioids, benzodiazepines, or cocaine is a type of polysubstance abuse and can increase the danger of building up a genuine alcohol issue.

Mixing alcohol with different drugs – including those recommended by a specialist – can prompt genuine wellbeing outcomes without taking appropriate consideration. For example, mixing alcohol with opioids, or even drugs for depression or anxiety can prompt negative side effects, for example, increased sedation, respiratory depression, and memory blackouts with large doses.

Binge Drinking

Binge drinking, which includes drinking an exorbitant measure of alcohol inside a short window of time, can likewise be a risk factor for alcoholism. For well-endowed individuals, this implies drinking at least five drinks in a setting, and at least four for ladies.

This degree of drinking is generally regular among young adults between the ages of 18 and 34. It's no fortuitous event that numerous individuals at this age are going to college and bound to get immersed in "party culture".

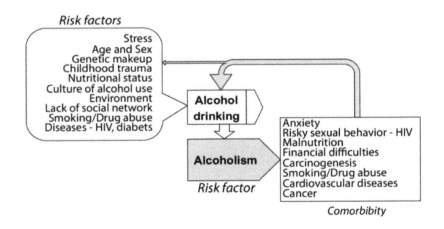

.

The Disease of Addiction

While there are numerous reasons that an individual may start to drink, individuals with the disease of alcoholism will locate those underlying reasons presently don't drive their drinking designs. At Starting points, we accept that alcoholism is a sickness that impacts the psyche, body, and spirit.

The Physical Allergy

At the point when the disease of alcoholism has grabbed hold, the alcoholic will start to drink more than they expect. Typical drinkers (people without alcoholism) will find that they are effectively ready to restrict the number of drinks that they burn-through. For the alcoholic, this may appear to be outlandish. They start to "lose all control of their liquor consumption once they start to drink." For them, the main drink sets off a hankering for more alcohol which can prompt a binge or gorge. This can bring about consequences that the individual might not have in any case experienced on the off danger that that they had the option to stop after the first drink.

The Mental Obsession

Even after an alcoholic has gone through medical detox and alcohol is not, at this point gift inside the frame, the disease of alcoholism is as yet grinding away. This is maybe the most wicked segment of the disease as it is hard to understand, in any event, for the alcoholic. Alcoholics who are caught in the pattern of fixation keep on getting back to the very substance that is obliterating their life. They may do this regardless of a staggering longing to stop drinking once and for all. For those confronting the sickness, determination alone isn't sufficient to remain sober. They become engrossed with the conviction that they can "control and enjoy" their drinking. Those of us in recuperation allude to this unusual mental bend as the "mental obsession."

It's an obsession to drink normally. An obsession to drink without consequences. An obsession to limit its destruction. An obsession to drink in secret wanting to trick the family, companions, and businesses who know precisely what the issue is.

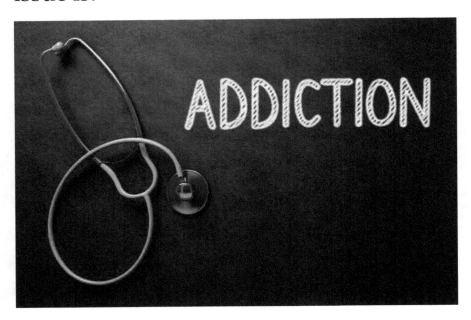

Why People Relapse?

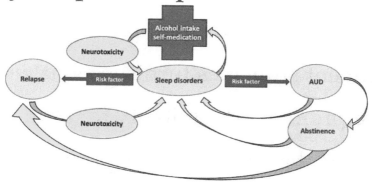

Remaining healthy and keeping up your sobriety requires significant investment and dedication. Shockingly, a few people relapse after alcohol treatment. Triggers, including a gathering of companions who drink, certain exercises or conditions can lead somebody to fall once again into old drinking habits.

Relapsing doesn't mean you've fizzled and can't beat alcoholism. It makes you mindful of triggers and may rouse you to look for extra assistance from a guide or care group. Participating in on-going treatment strategies furnishes you with a more prominent possibility for long-term sobriety than the individuals who don't proceed with recuperation with maintenance programs.

Reasons why some people relapse are:

- Old habits
- Stress and anxiety
- Social pressures
- Mental or emotional instability
- Anger or frustration
- Temptation to feel drunk again

Treatment is the initial move toward a superior tomorrow. Alcohol treatment experts work with you to make a customized far reaching recuperation plan with quantifiable objectives. Thorough recuperation plans may incorporate inpatient or outpatient treatment, prescription helped treatment, directing, and uphold gatherings.

9+1 Way to Quit drinking

1. Work out a plan

Regardless of whether you're meaning to drink less or to stop through and through, it's a smart thought to have an arrangement. A few people like to stop in one go. Others like to gradually decrease their drinking. Everybody is unique so work out what turns out best for you. Recollect that your primary care physician can help you in case you don't know. Your arrangement may be just about as straightforward as drinking one less glass each time you go out. In the event that you need to be more definite, have a consider your:

- Goals — why do you want to lessen or quit drinking?

- Triggers — why and when do you drink?

- Strategies — how will you reduce or quit alcohol?

- Support — who will you turn to for help?

Your goals

Having an unmistakable objective as a main priority can assist you with remaining inspired. Individuals lessen or stop alcohol for some, reasons, including to be better, to set aside cash, or to have more energy.

Your triggers

In case you don't know what your triggers are, it very well may be difficult to drink less. To work out why you're drinking alcohol, ask yourself the following questions:

· where are the spots, I drink the most?

· what times do I drink the most?

· would I like to drink or do I feel compelled?

When you know why you drink, you can work out approaches to stay away from circumstances where you may be enticed to drink.

Your strategies

Have a few systems set up so you're readied when you're enticed by alcohol. You'll realize what to do on the off chance that you surprisingly end up at an occasion where alcohol is being served.

It's a smart thought to keep away from your triggers to assist you with stopping or diminish alcohol. On the off chance that alcohol highlights in your public activity, you could:

- put together without alcohol occasions with your companions as opposed to going out for a beverage

- recommend settings where mocktails are accessible
- get up to speed over an espresso rather than at the bar
- mingle all the more frequently with companions who don't drink

Inside the event that you can't keep a strategic distance from your triggers, try to alternate the alcohol for something one of a kind. for example, on the off danger that you drink prior to going out to feel less on edge, get together with an old buddy all things considered.

Your support

In the same way as other things throughout everyday life, stopping or diminishing alcohol is a lot simpler with help. Educate your loved ones concerning what you're doing so they can help you. It's stunningly better on the off chance that you know somebody who is attempting to do something very similar. You can uphold one another.

2. Talk about it

Letting others realize approximately your desire to stop consuming may additionally help encourage you to stick with your choice.

Involve your loved ones

Loved ones can give consolation and backing when you quit ingesting. by way of opening up about your relationship with alcohol, you may likewise urge others to investigate their own drinking propensities. Possibly your partner, sibling, or roommate is likewise considering rolling out an improvement. Changing drinking propensities together permits you to help one another while additionally boosting your inspiration and responsibility. The person should take notes of the significance of bringing along a confided in help individual when going to occasions that include alcohol. It's frequently simpler to turn down a drink when you don't need to do it single-handedly.

Find a community

constructing new relationships with folks who additionally pick to avoid alcohol may have a whole lot of gain.

"The more help you've got, the better"

Here are some ideas:

- Rather than testing your determination by joining your co-workers for the standard party time, why not welcome an alternate co-specialist to look at the new bakery down the road?

- Consider developing friendship and romance with individuals who don't focus on drinking as a significant piece of their life.

- Miss the bar atmosphere? Contingent upon where you reside, you could possibly visit a sober bar and socialize without alcohol.
- test out apps like Meetup to find other humans interested in alcohol free activities.

Know what to say

whilst you turn down a drink, humans may ask why. you're now not obligated to provide info, however it may help to have a move-to reaction ready:

- "I am cutting back for my fitness."

- "I do not like the way consuming makes me experience."

All things considered, you don't have to say anything over "No, thanks." Practicing your refusal early can help you feel better and sure when you end up in a circumstance that includes alcohol. Make an effort not to stress over others judging you since the vast majority likely will not notice or recollect what you do. at the off chance that you want to offer friends and family a more nitty-gritty clarification however feels uncertain about what to say, it assists with keeping your clarification straightforward:

- "i have been ingesting plenty without a clear cause, and I want to spend some time rethinking that dependency."

- "I catch myself ingesting once I do not want to stand my feelings, and that I want to get higher at working thru them without alcohol."

- "I do not simply enjoy ingesting, and i am bored with doing it simply due to the fact anyone else does."

3. Change your environment

At the point when alcohol makes up a piece of your average everyday practice, drinking can become something of an automatic reaction, particularly when you feel overpowered. You should not have to totally rethink your life to stop drinking, yet a couple of changes in your surroundings can have a major effect.

Get rid of your alcohol

Alcohol in your home can tempt you when you're attempting to quit. on the off risk that you are feeling like a drink, realizing you'll need to go out and create a purchase can discourage you adequately long to locate a decent distraction. Save non-alcoholic drinks close by for yourself as well as other people. You don't have to bring to the table alcohol to be a decent host. Allow guests to bring their own alcohol — and take it with them when they leave. In the event that you live with roommates, consider requesting that they keep their alcohol far out rather than in shared open spaces.

Find a new favorite drink

Picking the correct substitution refreshment can help you stand firm in your craving to quit drinking. Plain water may offer a lot of health benefits, however, it's truly not the most intriguing decision. With a little imagination, you can discover something enjoyable that doesn't make you miss your favorite drink. Try:

- injecting plain or shining water with cleaved natural products or spices
- adding cinnamon sticks or flavors to tea, apple juice, or hot cocoa
- blending juice or lemonade in with shining water

Vary your routine

At the point when you will in general drink at a specific season of day, accomplishing something different is probably the most ideal approaches to break that design. Exercises that get you out of the house and moving regularly help most. Consider the following ideas:

- On the off chance that you typically meet companions for a drink after work, consider taking a walk or meeting them for a home base in the recreation center or other sans alcohol space.

- Rather than going to your typical eatery for supper and drinks, why not attempt another spot that doesn't serve alcohol? You'll will encounter something strange without feeling enticed to drink.

- Start cooking at home to occupy yourself and set aside some cash.

At the point when your craving to drink adjusts more to your temperament than a specific season of day, having a couple of elective adapting techniques prepared can help:

- Instead of taking a drink to calm anxiety, try affirmations, deep breathing, or meditation.

- Comfort yourself when feeling lonely by reaching out to a

loved one or watching a favorite movie.

4. Make time for self-care

Stopping drinking can feel pretty upsetting. In the event that you go to alcohol to oversee passionate distress, the additional overpower can incite the inclination to drink, causing accomplishment to appear to be considerably more unattainable. It's not unexpected to battle when rolling out huge improvements, yet great self-care practices can assist you with overseeing overpowering emotions and deal with your brain and body.

Prioritize wellness

Feeling at your best physically can support versatility and enthusiastic strength, preparing you to climate moves that trigger the longing to drink. By avoiding alcohol, you're stepping toward improving physical wellbeing. As you notice those medical advantages, you'll probably feel more invigorated and motivatedto keep up your advancement. Different tips to consider:

- Stay hydrated.
- Eat ordinary, adjusted suppers. Attempt to incorporate nourishments

that increment energy and lift temperament.

- Get ordinary active work, in case you're capable. Take a stab at climbing, cycling, moving, or roller-skating for charming approaches to remain dynamic.
- Focus on better rest. A decent objective for most grown-ups is 7 to 9 hours.

Rediscover hobbies

Numerous individuals use alcohol to adapt to weariness. Fulfilling leisure activities can divert you from wanting to drink, however, they likewise help you relax — something everybody needs to do. In case you've lately wound-up aching to get once more into an old hobby, presents an ideal opportunity to put it all on the line. Technology makes it simpler than at any other time to master new abilities and find innovative methods of interfacing, in any event, when you can't truly partake in exercises with others.

You also might try:

- Do-It-Yourself home activities
- building or painting models
- board or computer games
- chipping in
- sitting back with a decent book

Keep Record

Possibly you've never had any interest in logging your deepest thoughts, however journaling can be an incredible instrument to follow your emotions as you work on quitting alcohol. Investigating, recorded as a hard copy, what you find troublesome and when you most need to drink can help you notice designs that offer more understanding into your alcohol use. Contrasting the emotions that surface when you have a drink with the sentiments you experience while declining likewise causes you to perceive when drinking doesn't fix the issues you're attempting to oversee. A journal likewise offers a helpful space to list reasons you need to quit and brainstorm exercises to supplant drinking.

Explore new tools to cope

When you distinguish a portion of the primary reasons why you drink, you can start finding new techniques for tending to those triggers.

The most supportive way of dealing with stress frequently relies upon the conditions:

- At the point when you feel pitiful however need alone time, you should seriously think about a most loved collection or soothing book.

- At the point when you need to drink to evade relationship struggle or stress, you may vent to a family member or friend or practice better relational abilities to reconnect with your accomplice.

- On the off chance that forlornness triggers the craving to drink, you may investigate approaches to associate with removed companions or investigate approaches to fabricate new fellowships.

5. Reach out for support

Quitting alcohol all alone is harder for some than others, yet there's no compelling reason to go it single-handedly. In case you're struggling to adhere to your objective or simply need some additional guidance, consider connecting for proficient support. On the off chance that you feel good doing as such, raise your difficulties to your essential healthcare supplier. Finding a therapist can likewise be an extraordinary beginning stage on the off chance that you're not open to opening up to your healthcare supplier. It may likewise merit looking at a 12-venture program in your general vicinity, similar to Alcoholics Mysterious or Shrewd Recuperation, to check whether it seems like something that may be useful for you.

6. Drinking non-alcoholic drinks

In the realm of non-drinkers non-alcoholic beers, wines and spirits are Extremely questionable. Many contend they ought to be completely evaded as they are risky triggers, and just help individuals to remember what they're missing, consequently hauling them onto that tricky slant. However, for some others, myself notwithstanding, they're a lifeline.

On the off chance that an individual went through a few evenings in pubs drinking non-alcoholic beers and nobody has ever seen so he would be off the booze – handy if you need to dodge any abnormal inquiries, or can't be tried to guard your choice not to feel unpleasant the following day. It unquestionably feels like there's some sort of psychologically relieving impact of airing out that booze-free brew or popping that 'Nosecco' cork. We realized as of late that it takes alcohol seven minutes to hit the brain, so maybe it's not very unlike that fake introductory 'relief' you get when drinking the genuine article. Within the online groups we follow there have been numerous discussions about which ones are the awesome, are the ones that are most normally suggested by individuals aware of everything – alongside a couple of my favorites.

Note that most some are 0.5%. However, this is so low it's, in fact, viewed as AF (sans alcohol):

- BrewDog Babysitter State (0.5%) – broadly considered to the best non-alcoholic lager

- Nosecco (0.5%) – Numerous individuals like this, yet it tastes rather sweet.

- Crodino (0.0%)– We found this while on vacation in Italy. This non-alcoholic aperitif is an ideal option in contrast to a boozy Aperol Spritz!olic.

7. Make the most out of your hangover-free mornings

Perhaps the best thing about surrendering alcohol – close by better sleep, weight loss, clearer skin, and having more cash – is restoring the time you would've spent hungover on the couch. Presently you should've recovered your ends of the week, you ought to choose to benefit as much as possible from your recently discovered time and energy by running. we know it's not for everybody, but rather we'd recommend attempting to discover something you love that you had neither the time nor the energy for in the wake of drinking. It very well may be heating, doing a wellness DVD, or basically orchestrating all the earlier morning excursions with the children.

An individual began two or three years back however halted when his hangovers began enduring a few days. In those days, he was unable to run for over two minutes without needing a break – that is no distortion – yet, he slowly moved gradually up to 5k with the Couch to 5k digital recording. This is a splendid and FREE webcast of guided runs that progressively develop until before you know it you can run for 30 minutes ceaselessly. Indeed, even the super-incredulous author Charlie Brooker is a fan.

He proceeded onward from 5K and downloaded a running application by Verv. Alongside the 5K, it additionally incorporates other steady exercises to help you arrive at 10K, a half long-distance race, or a full long-distance race. In addition to the side of this one is you can pick between a lot of various soundtracks and it additionally tracks your distance, speed, GPS course, and calories consumed.

8. Build up your motivation to change

At the point when we directed our drinking from the outset, we monitored how we felt in the wake of drinking, so we could help ourselves to remember those negative effects before we began drinking. When we quit, we observed how much better we felt, making a point to see how composed we felt and how we felt a great deal more profitable in the mornings. From the outset, we didn't know we needed to stop by any means. Presently, we realize we'll never drink again, and we're so cheerful we did it. Over the long haul, our inspiration developed further instead of more fragile

9. Using Natural remedies to quit drinking

Albeit a basic glass of wine is useful for your cardiovascular wellbeing, in the event that you wind up gorging on in excess of a couple, you are putting your psychological and actual wellbeing at high danger. Indeed, an examination distributed in the diary Australian Therapist expresses that unreasonable drinking may prompt drunkorexia in young ladies. This is a harming and perilous practice where individuals miss dinners to repay the calorie consumption because of alcohol. Dieticians and specialists exhort carefully against this way of life because of its undeniable risks. You will positively experience the ill effects of different inadequacies as alcohol contains for all intents and purposes no wholesome substance other than void calories

- **Grapes:**

Quite possibly the most mainstream and normal approaches to control alcohol compulsion is having grapes. At whatever point you pine for a drink of alcohol, simply have a glass of grape squeeze or eat a lot of grapes all things being equal. Since they are the source from which wine is made, grapes fill in as an extraordinary option for weighty drinkers. Additionally, these natural products are wealthy in potassium, which causes your body to keep a basic blood balance, alongside invigorating the kidneys. Grapes can likewise purify poisons from the liver successfully.

• Fruit Juices

This common cure is something that works for some individuals. In the event that you are a solid alcoholic, you need to incorporate new, custom made juices in your eating regimen to dispose of your alcohol habit. These juices are loaded up with nutrient A, folate, nutrient C, calcium, magnesium, and potassium and can go about as an option at whatever point you want to have a drink.

• Date Juice

If you are engaging to adapt to alcohol enslavement, at that point have dates consistently. These organic products have certain properties which help in detoxifying and getting out poisons from your liver. Absorb a few dates water for one hour and later eliminate the seeds and crush them in the water. Have this drink two times each day for a very long time to accomplish the ideal outcomes.

- **Bitter Gourd Juice**

Severe gourd recuperates liver harm because of abundance alcohol utilization. This vegetable is a characteristic remedy that flushes out poisons from your body. To make the drink, separate juice from a couple of severe gourd leaves and blend 3 tsp in a glass of buttermilk. Have the blend on an unfilled stomach consistently for a couple of months to dispose of alcohol enslavement.

- **Carrot Juice**

Carrot is likewise one of the go-to fixings with regards to controlling the inclinations of drinking alcohol. This is because carrots have numerous medical advantages and supplements just as nutrients. At whatever point you want to drink alcohol, simply have a glass of carrot juice. This will cause you to feel better as it improves processing and treats alcohol fixation. Have a glass of carrot squeeze day by day to dispose of your alcohol longings.

10.   Don't Give Up

No place in this article did we say it is not difficult to quit drinking! Remember your objectives alongside the reasons you even set these objectives in any case. In the event that you have an lots of drinks one evening, don't allow it to ruin the objective you're going after. Simply get directly in the groove again the following day. At the point when you bomb yourself, simply recollect this statement by Robert F. Kennedy: "Just the individuals who try to flop extraordinarily can at any point accomplish significantly." You will succeed on the off chance that you really need to get your drinking propensities leveled out or quit drinking by and large.

Suppose that you have an objective to diminish your drinking, say it so anyone can hear like your companions or family, or even record it. Making a responsibility for all to hear or on paper implies you're substantially more liable to adhere to your objectives. Telling your loved ones can likewise help you feel more upheld as you make changes, and as you gain ground.

Conclusion

Alcohol is anything but a normal item. While it conveys undertones of joy and amiability in the personalities of many, hurtful results of its use are assorted and boundless

From a worldwide viewpoint, to decrease the mischief caused by alcohol, arrangements need to consider explicit circumstances in various social orders. Normal volumes burned-through and examples of drinking are two components of alcohol utilization that should be considered in endeavors to lessen the weight of alcohol-related issues. Keeping away from the mix of drinking and driving is an illustration of measures that can decrease the wellbeing weight of alcohol.

Public checking frameworks should be created to monitor alcohol utilization and its results and to bring issues to light among people in general and strategy producers. It is up to the two governments and concerned residents to empower discuss and plan powerful general wellbeing approaches that limit the mischief caused by alcohol.

The vast majority believe they're halting drinking since they're exhausted from feeling hangover. Or then again, they need to be better or set aside cash. On the whole, those are also great purposes behind stopping, yet they're likely not the simple explanation you're doing this. You're genuine 'why" goes a lot further than that – and this is actually what you need to tap into. To prevail with regards to lessening your drinking, you likewise need to break affiliations. For instance, in the event that you will, in general, reach for a drink when you get back home from work, plan an elective action to attempt to break this connection. It is essential to empower yourself en route.

Regardless of whether your advancement has been little, give yourself some acclaim.

Consider how you can remunerate yourself for the advancement you've made. For instance, on the off chance that you've set aside cash, could you treat yourself to something that you will appreciate, similar to a takeaway or some new garments? The best rewards are close to home to you and prompt.

CPSIA information can be obtained
at www.ICGtesting.com
Printed in the USA
BVHW051355080321
601998BV00011BA/1249